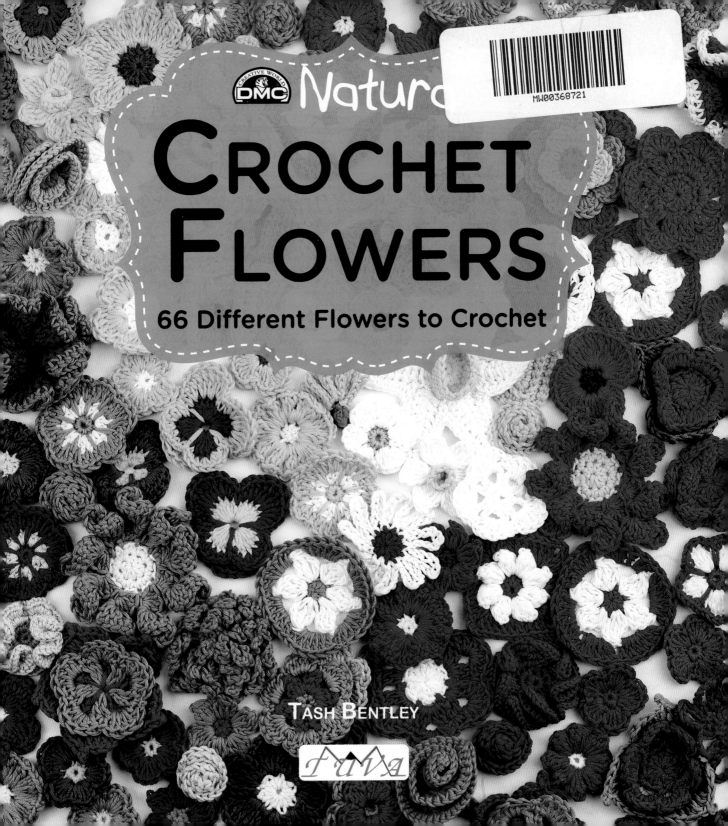

DMC CREATIVE WORLD

Nature

CROCHET
FLOWERS

66 Different Flowers to Crochet

TASH BENTLEY

Tuva

Tuva Publishing
www.tuvapublishing.com

Address: Merkez Mah. Cavusbasi Cad. No:71
Cekmekoy / - Istanbul 34782 / Turkey
Tel: 9 0216 642 62 62

Crochet Flowers

First Print: 2014 / January

All Global Copyrights Belongs To
Tuva Tekstil ve Yayıncılık Ltd.

Content: Crochet

Editor in Chief: Ayhan DEMİRPEHLİVAN
Project Editor: Kader DEMİRPEHLİVAN
Designer: Tash BENTLEY
Text Editor: Zoë HALSTEAD
Technical Advisor: K. Leyla ARAS
Graphic Design: Ömer ALP
Asistant: Kevser BAYRAKÇI

ISBN: 978-605-5647-53-7

Printing House
Bilnet Matbaacılık ve Yayıncılık A.Ş.

CONTENTS

MATERIALS AND EQUIPMENT

Hooks

Early crochet hooks were made of bone or wood with elaborately carved handles. Modern hooks are made from plastic, metal, bamboo or birch wood and come in a wide range of colours and shapes including soft or ergonomically shaped handles. There are even hooks with built in lights to enable crocheting in the dark.

Even sizes that are marked the same can vary between different manufacturers and style of hook. How you hold and use the hook can also impact on the sizing of your stitches. This is why it is always advisable to do several gauge swatches, trying out the yarn on different sized hooks.

Sizing of older hooks can be tricky as the size of the hook can vary from the neck down the shaft and there-fore stitch size can vary depending on where you crochet on the hook. A hook-sizing gadget (such as you would use to size knitting needles) is of little use in the sizing of these older hooks. The only true way to size them is to work with them.

Another thing to consider is the different methods used to size hooks in different countries and at different times. Older UK hooks were sized on a wool and a cotton (thread) numbering system and modern UK hooks on the millimetre system (eg 4mm, 4.5 mm...) whereas USA hooks are marked with a number or a letter that corresponds with its size in millimetres. The Japanese numbering system is different again and is not an exact match for either the UK or the USA systems of sizing. (See chart opposite). The millimetre method of marking hooks is slowly becoming the international standard.

No. 0 1.75mm
No. 2 1.50mm
No. 4 1.25mm
No. 6 1.00mm
No. 8 0.90mm
No. 10 0.75mm
No. 14 0.50mm

Hook Sizes Table

UK mm	US sizes	Japanese sizes	Older UK wool sizes	Older UK cotton sizes
2.00mm	-	0	14	1 1/2
2.25mm	1/B	-	13	-
2.50mm	-	1 (2.4mm)	12	0
2.75mm	C	2 (2.27mm)	11	-
3.00mm	-	3	11	3
3.25mm	D	4 (3.4mm)	10	-
3.50mm	4/E	5 (3.6mm)	9	4
3.75mm	F	6 (3.9mm)	-	-
4.00mm	6	7 (4.2mm)	8	5
4.25mm	G	-	-	-
4.50mm	7	8	7	-
5.00mm	8/H	9 (4.8mm) or 10 (5.1mm)	6	-
5.50mm	9/I	11 (5.4mm)	5	-
6.00mm	10/J	13	4	-
6.50mm	10.5/K	14 (6.3mm) or 15 (6.6mm)	3	-
7.00mm	-	7mm	2	-
8.00mm	11/L	8mm	0	-
9.00mm	13/M or N	9mm	00	-
10.00mm	15/N or P	10mm	000	-
12.00mm	P	-	-	-
16.00mm	Q	-	-	-

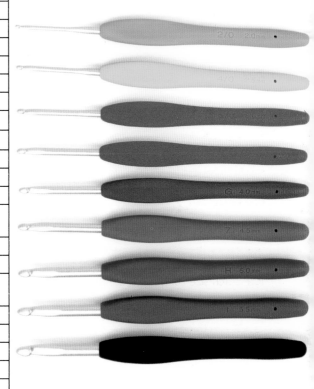

Wool Needle

A wool needle is essential for your crochet work to neatly sew in the ends of the yarn. Wool needles are larger than standard sewing needles and are made of metal or plastic with a blunt end and a large eye.

Yarn

Modern yarn comes in a wonderful range of colours and textures and can be made from a wide variety of materials including: wool, cotton, bamboo, acrylic, fabric, soya, and even plastic. Anything that makes a long flexible strip can be crocheted. The trick is to know what size of hook to use.

If using a commercially produced yarn then look at the ball band. This will give information on what the yarn is made of, weight, plus dye lot (for buying more of the exact same shade) and washing instructions. The manufacturer will also suggest hook and needle sizes for that particular yarn, but note that this is only a suggestion. Many interesting results can be produced by varying the size of hook used.

Yarn is produced in different thicknesses, known as weights, and can often be called 'ply'. Like hooks, these are described differently across the world. (See chart.)

Gauge

Because yarn weight varies greatly between manufacturers and between materials, the best way to decide the right hook and yarn for the chosen size of your project is to make a gauge swatch of the stitch pattern, varying the size of hook until you find the correct gauge. Gauge isn't vital for the patterns in this book but hook-to-yarn size will be. Experiment with both hooks and yarns to obtain results that please.

I have used Natura by DMC for all of the projects in this book. This is a 4ply cotton yarn sold in 50g balls and available in a wide selection of vibrant colours. DMC's Natura can be machine-washed and has a good stitch definition which adds to the look of the project.

You may, of course, use whatever yarns you have, but choose carefully. For example, some of the flowers with more structural shapes won't work in a very soft yarn as they will flop. To use a softer yarn it may be necessary to use a smaller hook to get the correct results. Again, experimenting is the key to creating a successful and pleasing result.

USA Yarn Number	USA Category	UK	Australia	Suggested hook size
0 Lace	Fingering, Thread	Lace, 1ply, 2ply	2ply, 3ply	2mm
1 Superfine	Sock, Fingering, Baby	4ply	5ply	2.25mm - 3.5mm
2 Fine	Sport, Baby	-	-	3.5mm - 4.5mm
3 Light	DK, Light Worsted	DK – Double Knitting	8ply	4.5mm - 5.5mm
4 Medium	Worsted, Afghan, Aran	Aran	10ply	5.5mm - 6.5mm
5 Bulky	Chunky, Craft, Rug	Chunky	12ply	6.5mm - 9mm
6 Super Bulky	Bulky, Roving	Super Chunky	14ply	9mm +

Stitchmarkers

These are useful for marking the last stitch on a round or to hold your place when you leave your work for a while. Also for marking that point in the work where you need to add a detail. Special stitchmarkers are available to use with crochet work, these have clasps that open which is essential. Crochet stitchmarkers are available in all styles from lovely handmade ones to simple split-ring plastic circles that slide onto the stitch. If you don't have any stitchmarkers handy then a short length of yarn in a different colour can be slipped in to mark the place, or a paperclip can be used.

STITCH LEGEND AND ABBREVIATIONS

ch - chain

dc - double crochet

MR - magic ring

dc2tog - double crochet 2 together

ch3picot - chain 3 picot

blo - work in back loop only

flo - work in front loop only

htr - half treble

htr spike - half treble spike

tr spike - treble spike

tr - treble crochet

tr2cl - treble 2 cluster

pc - popcorn

dtr - double treble

trtr - triple treble

tr5cl - treble 5 cluster

dtr2cl - double treble 2 cluster

tr3cl - treble 3 cluster

dtr4cl - double treble 4 cluster

dtr5cl - double treble 5 cluster

ss - slip stitch

foll – following
rep – repeat
sp – space
st(s) – stitch(es)
dtr3cl – double treble 3 cluster
ch2picot - chain 2 picot

8

DIRECTORY
OF
FLOWERS

4

3

2

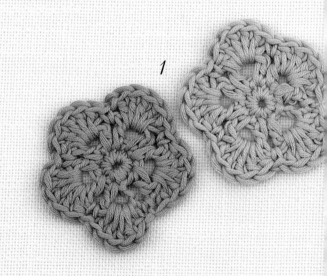

1

5

7

6

8

9

12

10

11

13

15

14

16

17

19

18

20

21

23

22

24

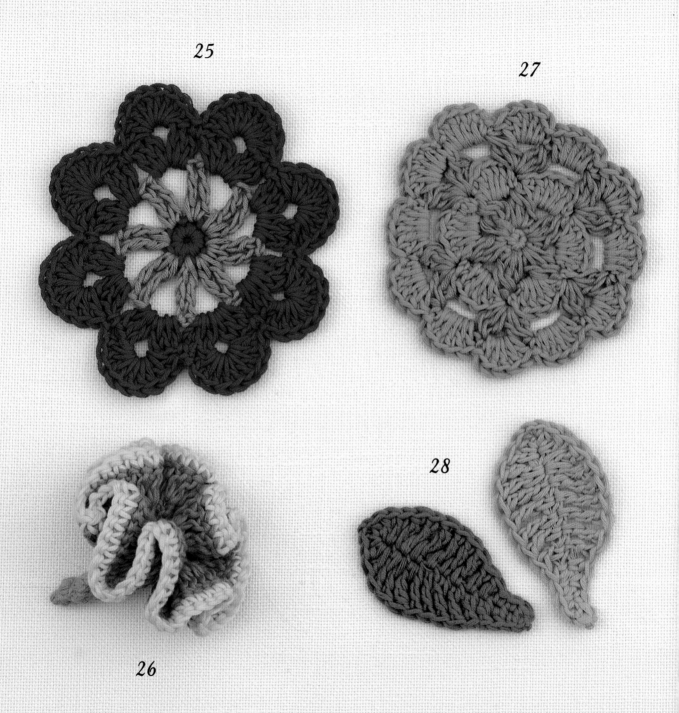

25

27

26

28

29

31

30

32

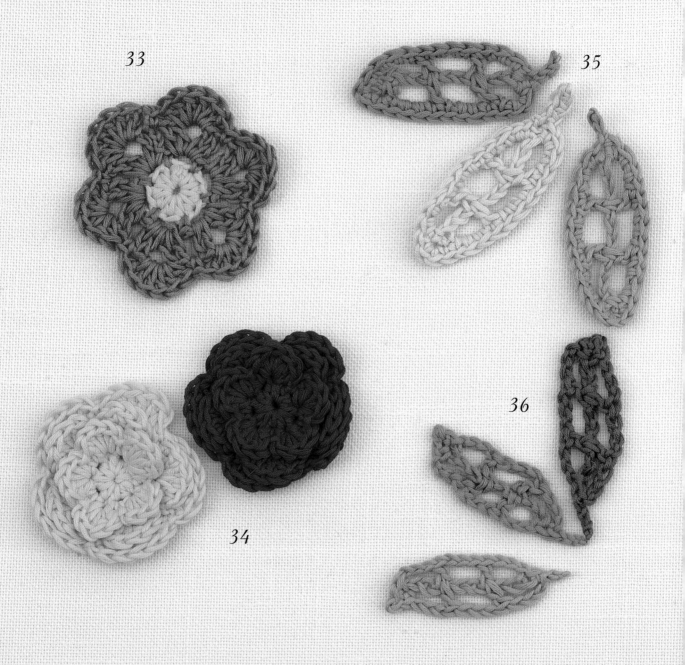

33

35

36

34

37

39

38

40

41

43

42

44

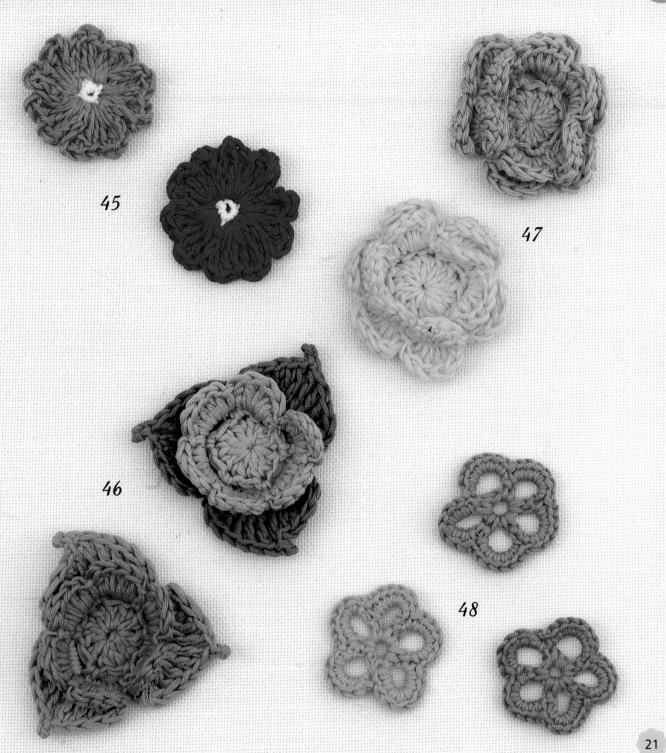

45

47

46

48

49

51

50

52

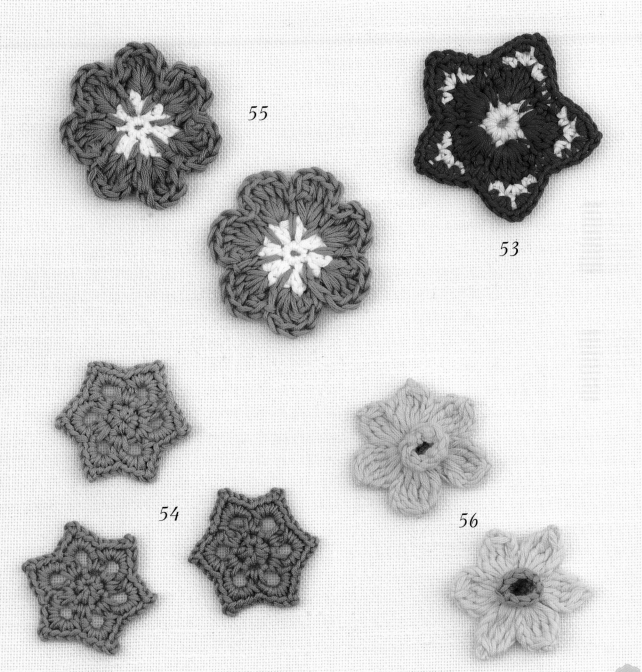

55

53

54

56

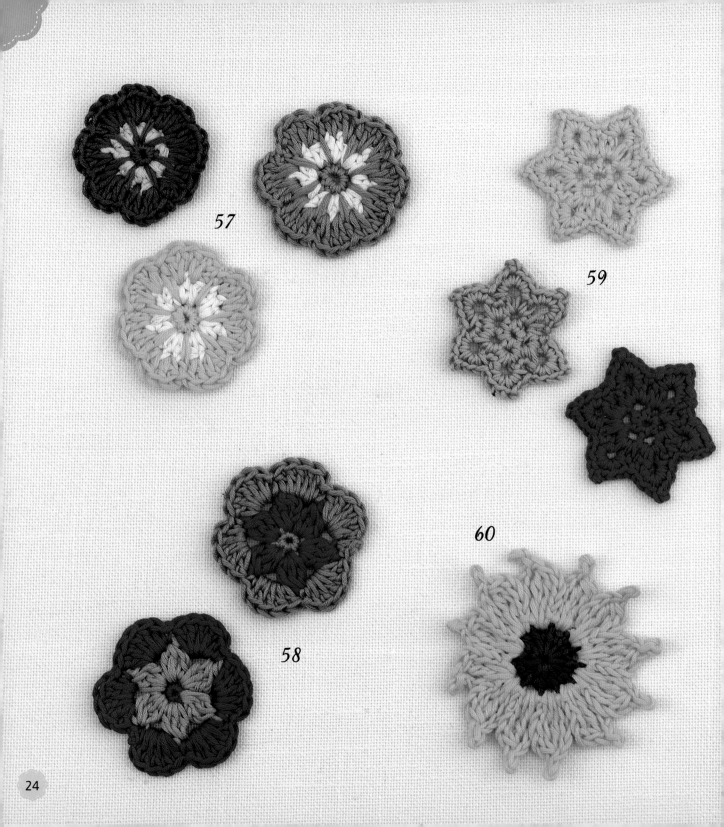

57

59

58

60

61

63

62

64

66

65

PROJECT
INSTRUCTIONS

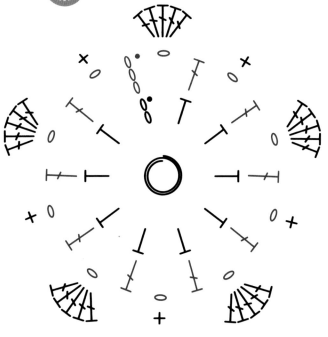

Worked in rounds

❀ MR, ch2, 9htr, join with ss

❀ ch4 (counts as 1tr and ch1), (1tr, ch1) into each htr, join with ss
in 3rd ch of ch4

❀ (1dc in ch1 sp, 5tr in foll ch1 sp) 5 times

❀ Fasten off, weave in ends

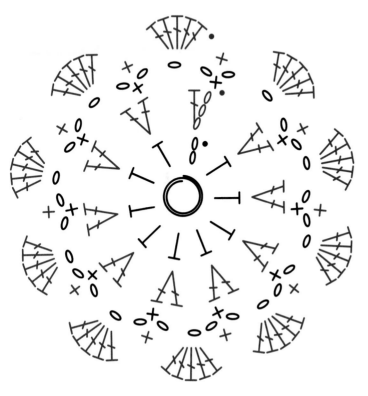

Worked in rounds

❀ in colour A, MR, ch2, 9htr into ring, join with ss, fasten off

❀ join colour B in any st, (ch3, 1tr) into same st, * 2tr into next st, rep from * 8 times more, join with ss in top of ch3, fasten off

❀ join colour A in any st, (ch3, miss 1 st, 1dc in next st) 10 times

❀ (5tr into ch3 sp, 1dc in dc) 10 times, join with ss

❀ Fasten off, weave in ends

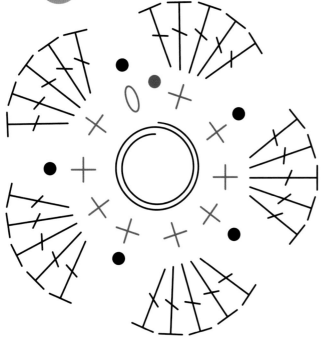

Worked in rounds

❀ in colour A, MR, ch1, 9dc into ring, join with ss, fasten off

❀ join colour B in any dc, * 5tr in next st, ss in foll st, rep from * 4 times more

❀ Fasten off, weave in ends

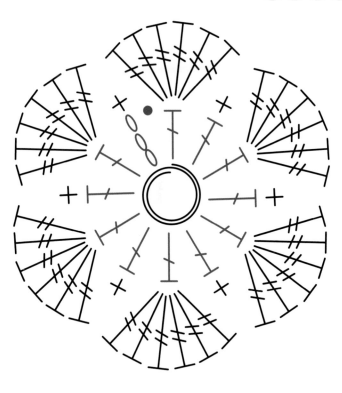

Worked in rounds

❀ in colour A, MR, ch3, 11tr into ring, join with ss, fasten off

❀ join colour B in any tr, * 6dtr in next st, dc in foll st, rep from *

5 times more

❀ Fasten off, weave in ends

5 6 Round Petal Flower - Medium

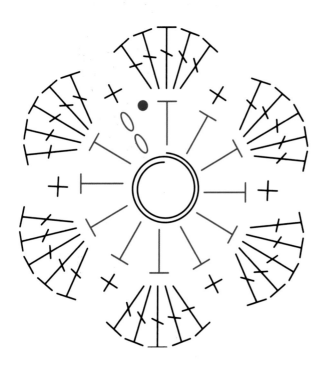

Worked in rounds

❀ in colour A, MR, ch2, 11htr into ring, join with ss, fasten off

❀ join colour B in any htr, * 5tr in next st, dc in foll st, rep from *
5 times more

❀ Fasten off, weave in ends

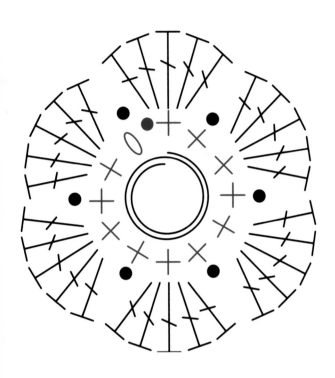

Worked in rounds

❀ in colour A, MR, ch1, 11dc into ring, join with ss, fasten off

❀ join colour B in any dc, * 5tr in next st, ss in foll st, rep from * 5 times more

❀ Fasten off, weave in ends

Bluebell

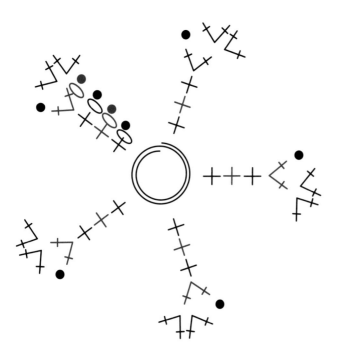

Worked in rounds

❀ MR, ch1, 5dc into ring, join with ss
❀ Ch1, 1dc in each dc, join with ss
❀ rep the last round once more
❀ ch1, 2dc in each dc, join with ss
❀ (4dc in next st, ss in foll st) 5 times
❀ Fasten off, weave in ends

Make several of the bluebell flowers and attach them to a stem, as shown, to make a spray of flowers.
Follow the instructions on page 117 to make stems.

Carnation Flower

8

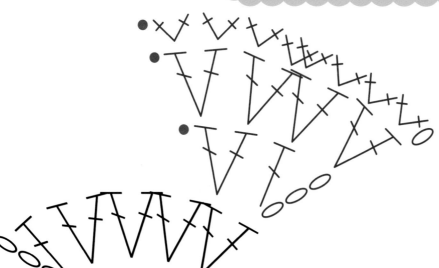

● Repeat to end

Work in rows

❀ in stem colour, ch3, work 5tr in 3rd ch from hook, ch3, turn

❀ work 1tr in same st as ch3, work 2tr in each st to end, change to petal colour before making ch3, turn

❀ work 1tr in same st as ch3, work 2tr in each st to end, ch3, turn

❀ work 1tr in same st as ch3, work 3tr in each st to end, change to petal edge colour before making ch1, turn

❀ work 2dc in each st to end

❀ Fasten off, weave in ends

❀ Roll up to form flower and sew in place

35

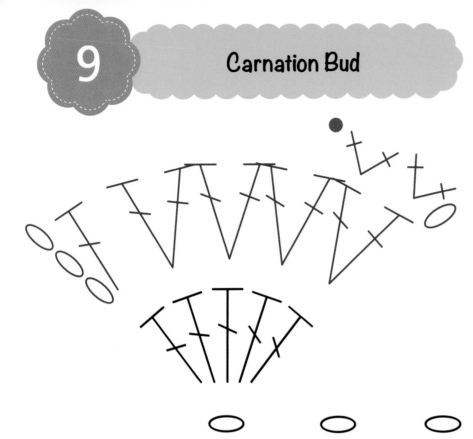

● Repeat to end

Work in rows

❀ in stem colour, ch3, work 5tr in 3rd ch from hook, change to bud colour before making ch3, turn

❀ work 1tr in same st as ch3, work 2tr in each st to end, change to bud edge colour before making ch1, turn

❀ work 2dc in each st to end

❀ Fasten off, weave in ends

❀ Roll up to form bud and sew in place

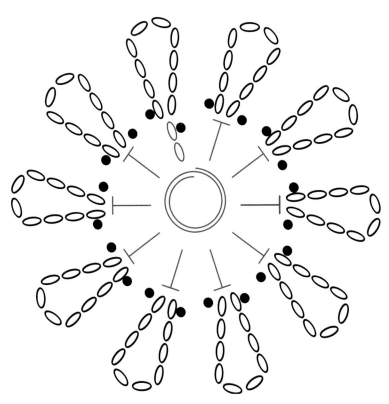

Worked in rounds

❁ MR, ch2, 9htr into ring, join with ss

❁ * ch10, ss in same st, ss in next st, rep from * 9 times more

❁ Fasten off, weave in ends

Chain Squiggle Flower Base

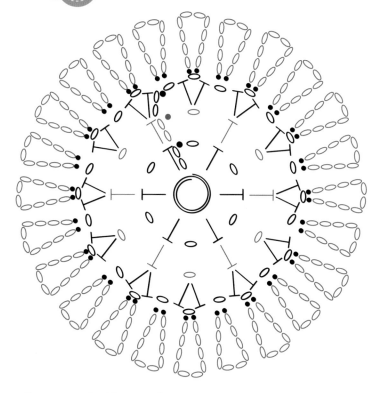

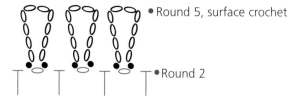

• Round 5, surface crochet

•Round 2

Base – worked in rounds

❀ MR, ch2, (1htr, ch1) 6 times into ring, join with ss

❀ ch2, * 1htr in top of htr, ch1, miss ch1 in round below, rep from * 5 times more, join with ss

❀ ch2, (work (1htr, ch1, 1htr, ch1) into each htr and ch1 sp) 12 times, join with a ss

❀ ss in ch1 sp, *ch10, ss in same ch1 sp, ss in next ch1 sp, rep from * 23 more times

Petals worked as surface crochet into the ch1 sp in the base

❀ ss in ch1 sp in round 2, *ch10, ss in same ch1 sp, ss in next ch1 sp, rep from * working in a spiral until all the ch1 sp from rounds 3-1 have a chain loop worked into them

❀ Fasten off, weave in ends

Worked in rounds

❁ in colour A, MR, ch1, 11dc into ring, join with ss

❁ * work 5tr in next dc, 1dc in foll dc, rep from * 5 times more, fasten off

❁ join colour B in blo of 3rd tr in 5tr petal, * ch3, dc in blo of 3rd tr of next 5tr petal, rep from * 5 times more

❁ ss into next ch3 sp, (ch3, 4tr) in same sp, * 5tr in next ch3 sp, rep from * 4 times more, join with ss in top of ch3

❁ Fasten off, weave in ends

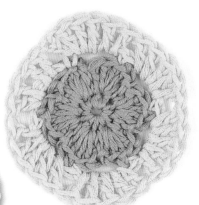

Clematis

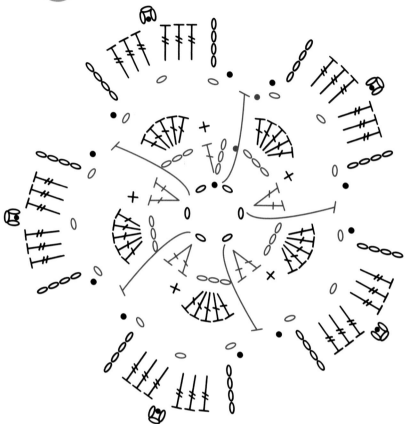

Worked in rounds

❀ in centre colour, ch6, join with ss to form a ring

❀ ch3, 1tr, ch3, (2tr, ch3) 4 times into ring, join with ss in top of first ch3

❀ (work 5tr in next ch3 sp, miss 1 st, 1dc in next st) 5 times, fasten off

❀ join outer colour to back of tr from round 3, working behind the petals, (htr spike into ring of round 1 between 2tr from round 2, ch3) 5 times, ss to first htr spike

❀ (ss in next ch3 sp, ch4, 3dtr, ch3 picot, 3dtr, ch4, ss in same sp) 5 times

❀ Fasten off, weave in ends

Worked in rows

❀ Ch9, 7tr into 3rd ch from hook, 7tr in each ch to end

❀ Allow to curl and ss into 1tr to close the base

❀ Fasten off, weave in ends

15 Curled Petal Flower

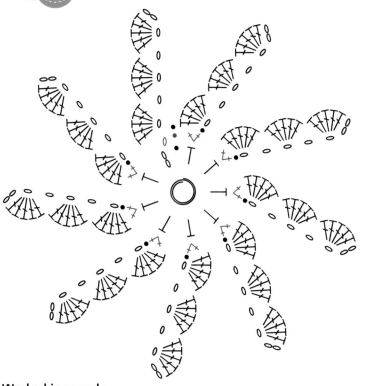

Worked in rounds

❀ in centre colour, MR, ch2, 8htr into ring, join with ss

❀ ch1, 1dc in same st, (2dc in each htr) 8 times, join with ss

❀ join petal colour, * ch7, work 5tr in 3rd ch from hook, (miss 1 ch, 5tr in next ch) twice, miss 1dc, ss in next dc *, rep from * to * 8 times more

❀ Fasten off, weave in ends

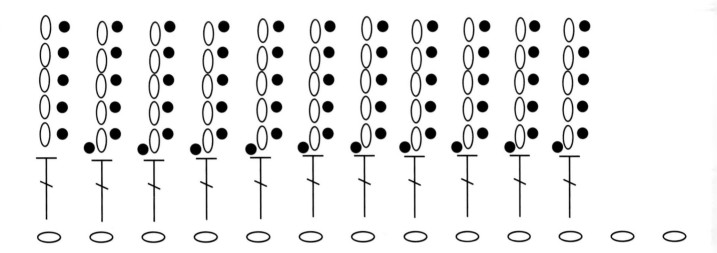

Worked in rows

❋ in green, ch13, work 1tr in 3rd ch from hook, work
1tr in each ch to end, fasten off

❋ join yellow, * ch5, ss back down ch5, ss in next tr,
rep from * to end.

❋ Roll up and sew into place

❋ Fasten off, weave in ends

Dandelion Flower

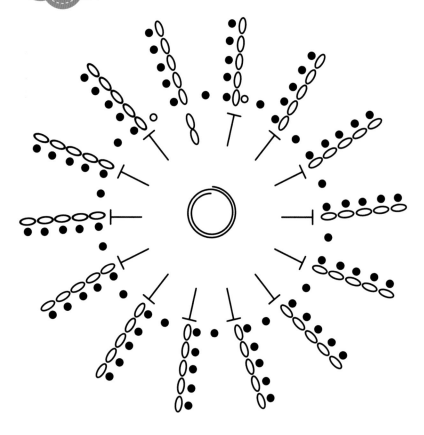

Worked in rounds

❀ in yellow, MR, ch2, 13htr into ring, join with ss

❀ * ch5, ss back down ch5, ss in next htr, rep from

* 13 times more

❀ Fasten off, weave in ends

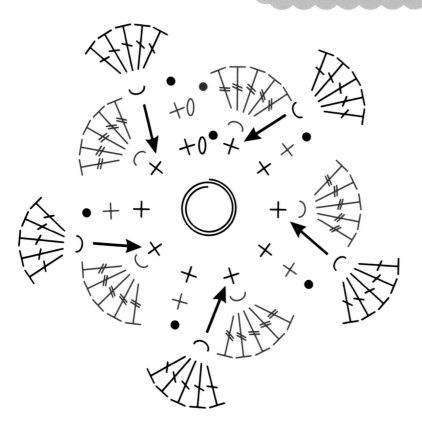

Worked in rounds

❀ in color A, MR, ch1, 10dc into ring, join with ss

❀ ch1, (1dc in dc, 5dtr in blo of next dc) 5 times, ss in first dc, fasten off

❀ join color B in flo of petal just worked, (5tr in flo, ss in next dc) 5 times

❀ Fasten off, weave in ends

Fuchsia

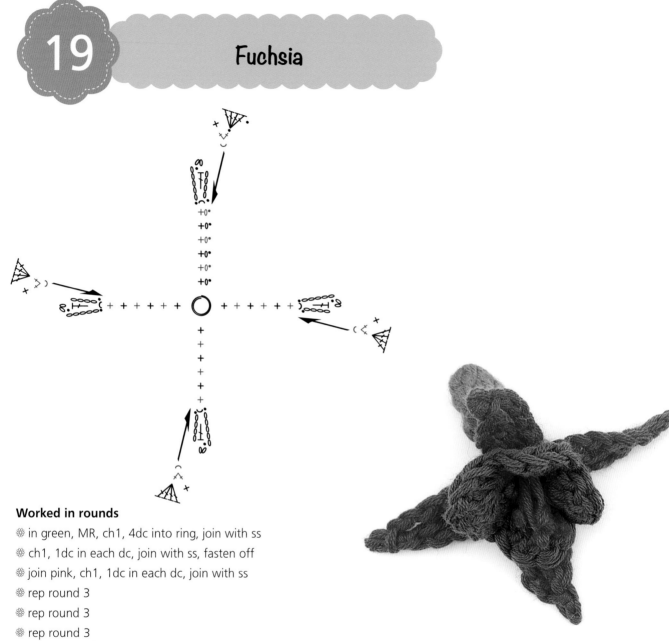

Worked in rounds

❀ in green, MR, ch1, 4dc into ring, join with ss

❀ ch1, 1dc in each dc, join with ss, fasten off

❀ join pink, ch1, 1dc in each dc, join with ss

❀ rep round 3

❀ rep round 3

❀ rep round 3

❀ * (ch4, 1tr, ch2 picot, ch5, ss) in blo of next dc, ss in next dc, rep from * 3 times more, fasten off

❀ join purple to flo of any dc from round 6, (2dc into flo of dc) 4 times, join with ss

❀ (4tr in next dc, 1dc in foll dc) 4 times, join with ss

❀ Fasten off, weave in ends

Take 2 strands of pink, fold them in half and secure inside centre of the flower, tie knots in the ends and trim.

● Repeat

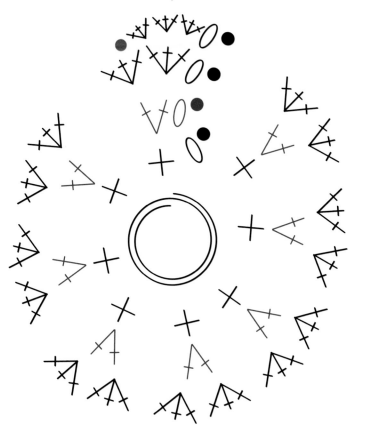

Worked in rounds

❀ in color A, MR, ch1, 8dc into ring, join with ss

❀ ch1, (2dc in each dc) 8 times, join with ss, fasten off

❀ join color B, ch1, (3dc in each dc) 16 times, join with ss

❀ ch1, (3dc into each dc) 48 times, join with ss

❀ Fasten off, weave in ends

Worked in rounds

❀ MR, ch1, 8dc into ring, join with ss

❀ ch1, * 2dc in each dc, rep from * to end, join with ss

❀ rep round 2 until flower is desired size

❀ Fasten off, weave in ends

Tip: Use a hook 1/2-1 size smaller than your yarn recommends.

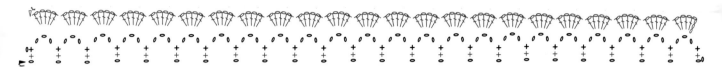

Worked in rows

❀ ch25, make first dc in 2nd ch from hook, 1dc in each ch to end, turn

❀ ch1, 1dc in dc, (ch3, 1dc in dc) to end, turn

❀ in ch3 sp work ch4 (counts as 1tr 1ch), 1tr, (ch1, 1tr) 3 times, * in next ch3 sp work 1tr, (ch1, 1tr) 4 times, rep from * to end

❀ Fasten off leaving a long tail to sew up

Roll into flower shape, sewing to secure in place as you roll.
To vary the size of the flower, make the starting chain longer.

23 Large Centre, Small Petals Flower

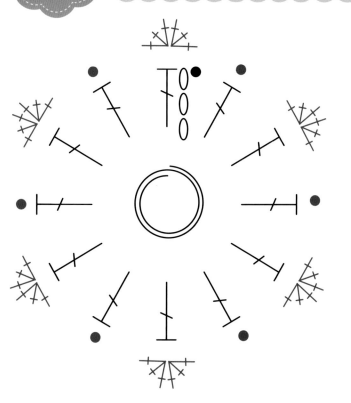

Worked in rounds

❈ in colour A, MR, ch3, 12tr into ring, join with ss
❈ join colour B, (6dc in next tr, ss in foll tr) 6 times
❈ Fasten off, weave in ends

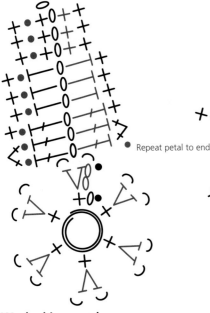

Repeat petal to end

Trumpet

Worked in rounds
Base and petals

❀ MR, ch1, 6dc into ring, join with ss

❀ ch2, (2htr in each dc) 6 times, join with ss in blo

❀ * ch10, work first dc in 2nd ch from hook, 1dc in each of next 2ch, 1htr in each of next 3ch, 1tr in each of next 3ch to bottom, miss 1 st in round, ss in blo of next st, rep from * 5 times more

❀ * working up opposite side of ch, 1tr in each of next 3ch, 1htr in each of next 3ch, 1dc in each of next 3ch, ss in each of next 10 sts of round 3 down petal, rep from * 5 times more

❀ * dc2tog, 1dc in each of next 7 sts, 3dc in next st (turning the corner at the point of the petal), 1dc in each of next 7 sts, dc2tog, rep from * 5 times more

❀ Fasten off, weave in ends

Worked in rounds
Trumpet

❀ join yarn in flo of round 2 of base, ch1, * 1dc in each flo, rep from * 11 times, join with ss

❀ ch1, * 1dc in each dc, rep from * to end, join with

❀ rep the last round 3 times more

❀ Fasten off, weave in ends

25 Large Flower Motif

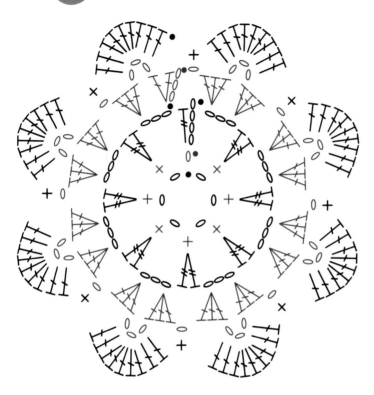

Worked in rounds

❀ in colour A, ch6, join with ss to make a ring

❀ ch1, 7dc into ring, join with ss

❀ join colour B, ch4, 1dtr in same st, ch3, * 2dtr, ch3, rep from * in each dc, join
with ss in top of ch4

❀ ss into next ch3 sp, (ch3, 2tr, ch3, 3tr, ch1) all in ch3 sp, * (3tr, ch3, 3tr, ch1) all
in next ch3 sp, rep from * 6 times more, join with ss in top of first ch3

❀ (9tr into next ch3 sp, 1dc into ch1 sp) 8 times, join with ss

❀ Fasten off, weave in ends

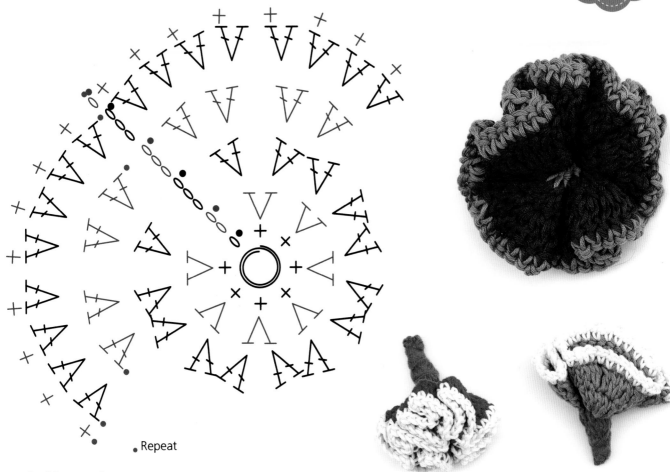

. Repeat

Worked in rounds

❋ in stem colour, MR, ch1, 7dc into ring, join with ss

❋ ch2, * 2htr in each dc, rep from * to end, join with ss

❋ ch3, * 2tr in each htr, rep from * to end, join with ss, fasten off leaving a long length for sewing up

❋ join flower colour, ch3, * 2tr in each tr, rep from * to end, join with ss

❋ rep last round, fasten off

❋ join edge colour, ch1 * 1dc in each tr, rep from * to end, join with ss

❋ Fasten off

Pinch into a rough cone and sew in place at end of round 3.
Wrap the yarn around the green section to make a stem.

27 Large Star and Round Flower Motif

Worked in rounds

❀ in colour A, MR, ch1, 6dc into ring, join with ss, fasten off

❀ join colour B to any dc, ch3, tr2cl, ch3, * tr3cl, ch3, rep from * 5 times more, join with ss in top of ch3, fasten off

❀ rejoin colour A to top of any tr3cl, ch1, 1dc in same st, 5tr into ch3 sp, * 1dc in top of next tr3cl, 5tr into ch3 sp, rep from * 5 times more, join with ss to ch1, fasten off

❀ rejoin colour B in any dc, (ch3, tr2cl, ch3, tr3cl) all into dc, ch3, * (tr3cl, ch3, tr3cl) all into next dc, ch3, rep from * 4 times more, join with ss in top of ch3, fasten off

❀ rejoin colour A to top of any tr3cl, ch1, dc in same st, 5tr into 3ch sp, * 1dc in top of tr3cl, 5tr in next ch3 sp, rep from * 10 times more, join with ss in ch1

❀ Fasten off, weave in ends

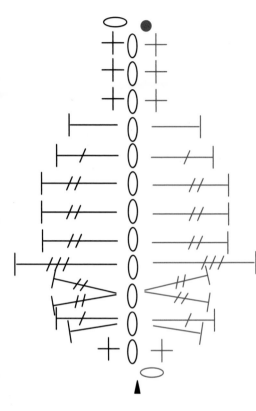

Worked in rows up both sides of a single chain

❀ ch13, work 1dc in 2nd ch from hook, 1dc in each of next 2sts, 1htr in next ch, 1tr in foll ch, 1dtr in each of next 3 ch, 1trtr in next ch, 2dtr in foll ch, (1tr, 1htr) in next ch, 1dc in end ch

❀ working along the opposite side of ch, ch1, 1dc in next ch, (1htr, 1tr) in next ch, 2dtr in foll ch, 1trtr in next ch, 1dtr in each of next 3 ch, 1tr in foll ch, 1htr in next ch, 1dc in each of next 3 ch, ss in end

❀ Fasten off, weave in ends

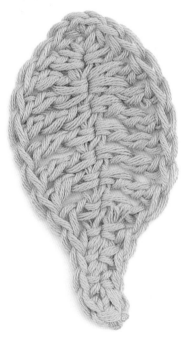

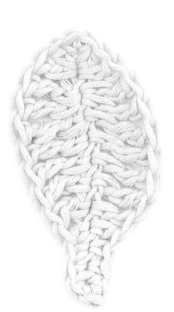

Water Lily Pad

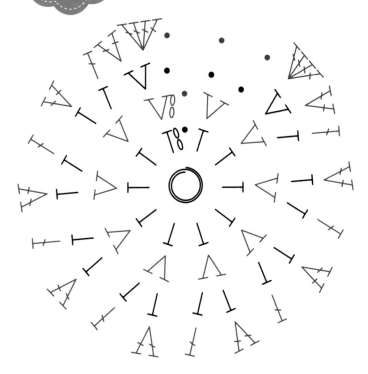

Worked in rounds

❀ MR, ch2, 10htr into ring, join with ss

❀ ch2, * 2htr in each htr, rep from * to end, join with ss

❀ 2htr in next st, 1htr in each of next 15 sts, 2htr in next st, ss in each of next 3 sts

❀ 4tr into next st, 2tr in foll st, (1tr in next st, 2tr in foll st) 8 times, 4tr in next st, ss in each of next 3 sts

❀ Fasten off, weave in ends

Look Page 93 for Water Lily.

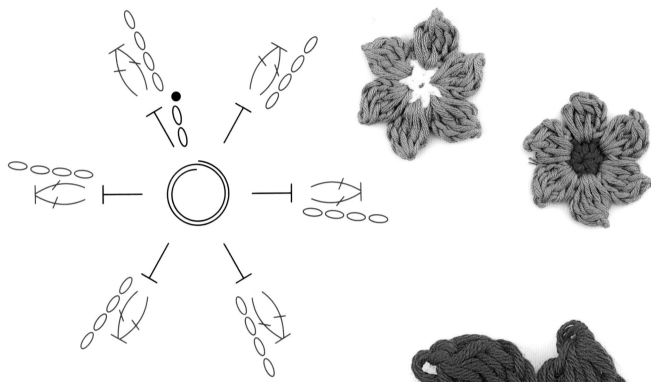

Worked in rounds

❈ in colour A, MR, ch2, 6htr into ring, join with ss, fasten off

❈ join colour B in any st, (ch4, tr2cl) in each htr

❈ Fasten off, weave in ends

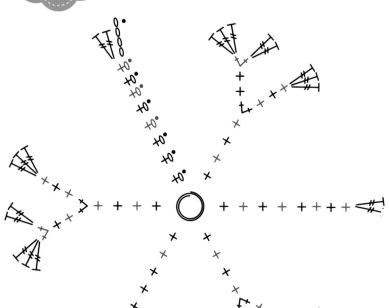

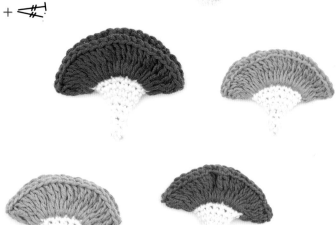

Worked in rounds

❀ in white, MR, ch1, 6dc into ring, join with ss

❀ ch1, * 1dc in each dc, rep from * to end, join with ss

❀ rep round 2

❀ rep round 2

❀ ch1, (1dc in next dc, 2dc in foll dc) 3 times, join with ss

❀ rep round 2

❀ rep round 2

❀ ch1, (1dc in each of next 2 dc, 2dc in foll dc) 3 times, join with ss, fasten off

❀ join colour in any st, ch4, (2dtr in next dc, 3dtr in foll dc) 6 times

❀ Fasten off, weave in ends

Worked in rounds

❀ in colour A, MR, ch2, 9htr into ring, join with ss into flo

❀ 1dc in flo of same st as ss, 5tr in flo of next htr, (1dc in flo of next htr, 5tr in foll htr) 4 times, join with ss in first dc, fasten off

❀ join colour B in blo of any st in round 1, (ch2, 1htr) in blo of htr, (2htr in blo of next htr) 9 times, join with ss in top of ch2

❀ rep round 2, fasten off

❀ join colour C in blo of any st in round 3, (ch2, 1htr) in blo of htr, 1htr in blo of htr, (2htr in blo of next htr, 1htr in blo of foll htr) 9 times, join with ss in top of ch2

❀ rep round 2 working into both loops

❀ Fasten off, weave in ends

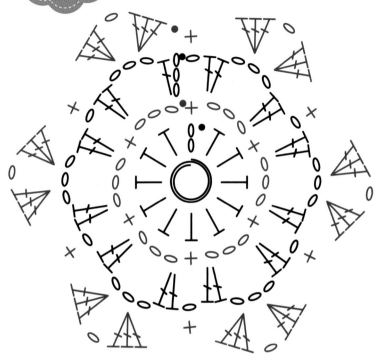

Worked in rounds

❀ MR, ch2, 11htr into ring, join with ss in top of ch2

❀ (ch3, miss 1 st in round below, 1dc in next htr) 6 times

❀ ss into ch3 sp, (ch3, 1tr, ch3, 2tr, ch1) all into ch3 sp, * (2tr, ch3, 2tr) all into ch3 sp, ch1, rep from * 4 times more, join with ss in top of ch3

❀ * (3tr, ch1, 3tr) into ch3 sp, 1dc into ch1 sp, rep from * 5 times more, join with ss

❀ Fasten off, weave in ends

Variation – change the colour of the centre by working round 1 in a different colour

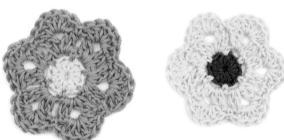

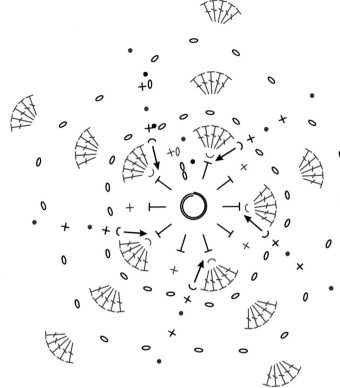

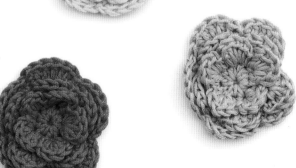

Worked in rounds

❋ MR, ch2, 9htr into ring, join with ss

❋ ch1, 1dc in same st, 5tr in flo of next htr, (1dc in next htr, 5tr in flo of next htr) 4 times, join with ss in ch1

❋ ss in blo of next htr of round 1 (behind petals just worked), 1dc in same blo of htr, ch4, (1dc in blo of next htr, ch4) 4 times

❋ (5tr in ch4 sp, ss in dc) 5 times

❋ ch1, 1dc in same st, ch4, (1dc in ss, ch4) 4 times, join with ss in ch1

❋ (5tr in ch4 sp, ss in dc) 5 times

❋ Fasten off, weave in ends

35 Outline Leaf

Worked in rounds around a central chain

❀ ch12, make ss in 2nd ch from hook, (ch3, miss 2 ch, 1tr in next ch) twice, ch3, miss 2 ch, 1dc in next ch, ss in last ch

❀ work along the opposite side of ch as follows: ss in first ch, 1dc in next ch, (ch3, miss 2 ch, 1tr in next ch) twice, ch3, miss 2 ch, ss in last ch, ch4 for stem

❀ make ss in 2nd ch from hook, ss in each of next 2 ch, 1dc in next st, (work 3dc into ch3 sp, 1dc in top of tr) twice, 3dc in ch3 sp, 1dc in next st, 3dc in next st (to make point), 1dc in next st, (3dc into ch3 sp, 1dc in top of tr) twice, 3dc in ch3 sp, 1dc in next st

❀ Fasten off, weave in ends

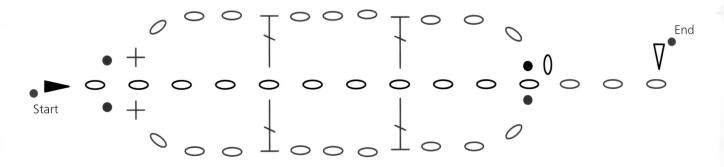

Start

End

Worked in rows around a central chain

❀ ch12, make ss in 2nd ch from hook, (ch3, miss 2 ch, 1tr in next ch) twice, ch3, miss 2 ch, 1dc in next ch, ss in last ch

❀ work along the opposite side of ch as follows: ss in first ch, 1dc in next ch, (ch3, miss 2 ch, 1tr in next ch) twice, ch3, miss 2 ch, ss in last ch, ch3 for stem

❀ Fasten off, weave in ends

Pansy

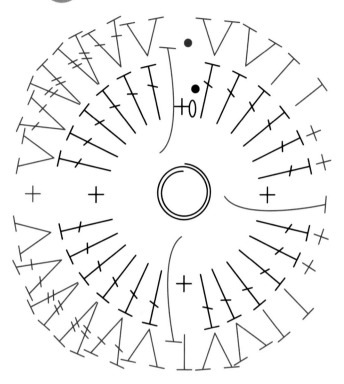

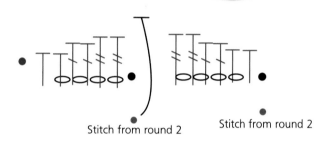

Stitch from round 2   Stitch from round 2

Worked in rounds

❈ in centre colour, MR, ch1, (1dc, 6tr) 4 times into ring, join with ss in top of first dc, fasten off

❈ join outer colour to dc, htr spike into ring, * 2htr in next st, 2tr in next st, 2dtr in each of next 2 sts, 2tr in next st, 2htr in foll st *, 1dc in dc, rep from * to * in next 6 sts, htr spike into ring, 1htr in dc, 2htr in each of next 2 sts, 1htr in each of next 2 sts, 1dc in each of next 2 sts, htr spike into ring, 1dc in each of next 2 sts, 1htr in each of next 2 sts, 2htr in each of next 2 sts, join with ss in top of htr spike

❈ working behind petals, ch4, ss in back of last htr spike from last round, ch4, ss in dc from last round

❈ work (2htr, 2tr, 2dtr) all into ch4 sp just made, then work (2dtr, 2tr, 2htr) all in other ch4 sp

❈ Fasten off, weave in ends

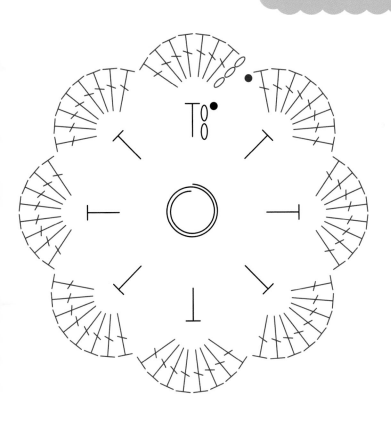

Worked in rounds

❁ in centre colour, MR, ch2, 8htr into ring, join with ss, fasten off

❁ join petal colour, ch3, 7tr in htr, * 8tr in next htr, rep from * 6 times more, join with ss in top of ch3

❁ Fasten off, weave in ends

39 Picot Edged Motif

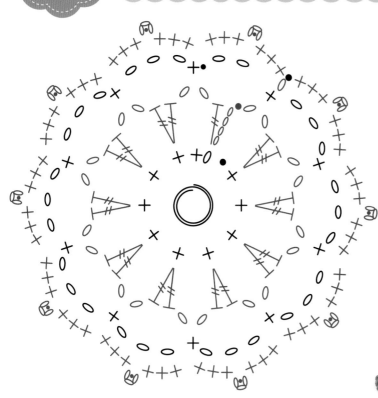

Worked in rounds

❀ in colour A, MR, ch1, 10dc into ring, join with ss, fasten off

❀ join colour B, ch4, dtr in same st, ch2, (2dtr in next dc, ch2) 9 times, join with ss, fasten off

❀ rejoin colour A, (1dc in ch2 sp, ch3) 10 times, join with ss

❀ ((3dc, ch3picot, 3dc) all in ch3 sp) 10 times

❀ Fasten off, weave in ends

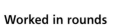

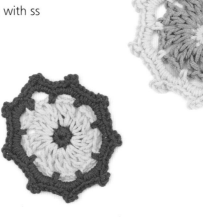

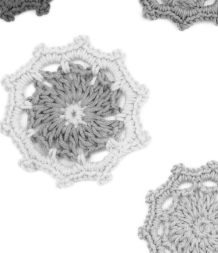

66

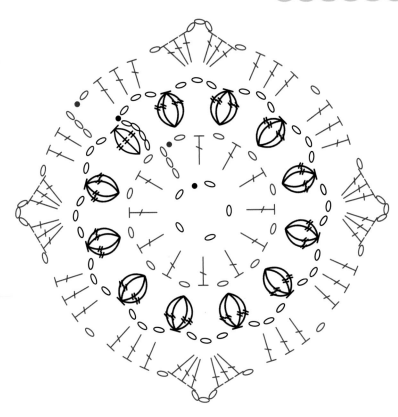

Worked in rounds

❀ ch5, join with ss to make a ring

❀ ch4 (counts as 1tr and 1ch), (1tr, ch1) 11 times, join with ss in 3rd ch of ch4

❀ ss in ch1 sp, ch4, work dtr3cl into ch1 sp, ch3, (dtr4cl into next ch1 sp, ch3) 11 times, join with ss in top of ch4

❀ ss in ch3 sp, (ch3, 2tr, ch1) into ch3 sp, * (3tr, ch3, 3tr) into ch3 sp (corner made), ch1, (3tr, ch1) in each of next 2 ch3 sp, rep from * twice more, (3tr, ch3, 3tr) into next ch3 sp, (3tr, ch1) in last ch3 sp, join with ss in top of ch3

❀ Fasten off, weave in ends

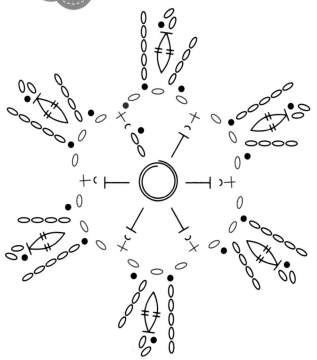

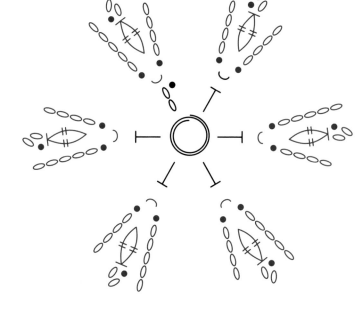

Worked in rounds

❀ in yellow, MR, ch2, 5htr into ring, join with ss, fasten off

❀ join red in blo of any st, (1dc in blo, ch3) 6 times, join with ss in dc

❀ (ss in next ch3 sp, ch4, dtr2cl, ch2picot, ch5, ss in same ch3 sp) 6 times

❀ (ss in flo of next htr from round 1, ch4, dtr2cl, ch2picot, ch5, ss in same flo of htr) 6 times

❀ Fasten off, weave in ends

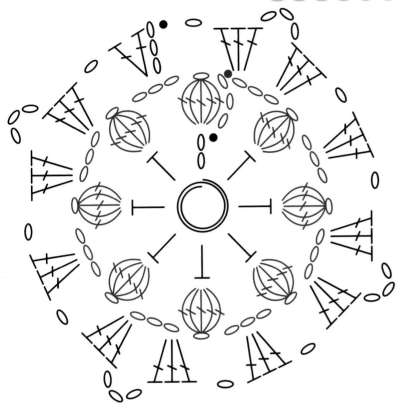

Worked in rounds

❉ in centre colour, MR, ch2, 7htr into ring, join with ss, fasten off

❉ join petal colour in any st, ch3, (PC, ch3) 8 times, join with ss in ch3, fasten off

❉ join outer colour in any ch3 sp, (ch3 (counts as 1tr), 2tr, ch1) into ch3 sp, * (3tr, ch3, 3tr, ch1) into next ch3 sp (corner made), (3tr, ch1) in foll ch3 sp, rep from * twice more, (3tr, ch3, 3tr, ch1) in next ch3 sp, join with ss in top of first ch3

❉ Fasten off, weave in ends

These cute little squares would be ideal to join together to make into a larger project. I think they would look lovely as a cushion cover.

Worked in rounds

❀ in centre colour, MR, ch2, 7htr into ring, join with ss, fasten off
❀ join petal colour in any st, ch3, (PC, ch3) 8 times, join with ss in ch3
❀ Fasten off, weave in ends

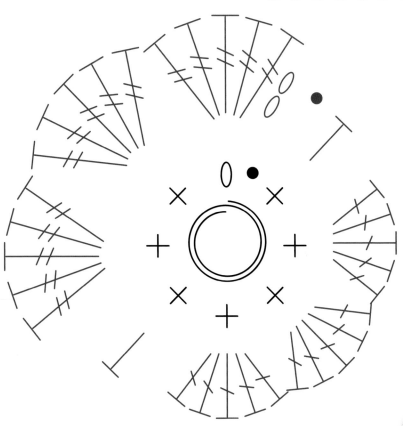

Worked in rounds

❀ in brown, MR, ch1, 7dc into ring, join with ss, fasten off

❀ join red in any st, ch2, 5dtr in each of next 3 sts, 1htr in foll st, 5tr in each of next 3 sts, 1htr in foll st, join with a ss in ch2

❀ Fasten off, weave in ends

Primula

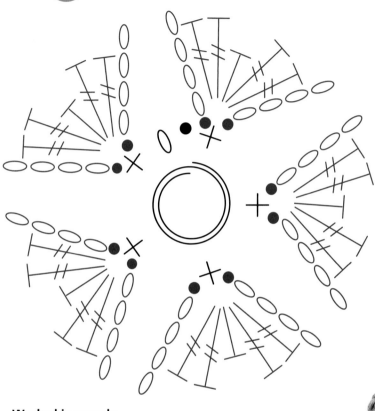

Worked in rounds

❀ in centre colour, MR, ch1, 5dc into ring, join with ss, fasten off

❀ join petal colour in any st, * ss in next st, (ch4, 2dtr, 1htr, 2dtr, ch4, ss) all in same st, rep from * 4 times more

❀ Fasten off, weave in ends

Round 4
Round 3
Round 5

Worked in rounds

❀ in flower colour, MR, ch2, 11tr into ring, join with ss

❀ (ch3, miss 1 st, 1dc in next st) 6 times

❀ (ch3, miss ch3, ss in dc) 6 times

❀ ((ss into next ch3 sp, 5tr, ss) all into ch3 sp) 6 times, fasten off

❀ Join leaf colour with ss into ch3 sp of round 2, * 6dtr, ch3picot, (6dtr, ss) into next ch3 sp, ss into next ch3 sp, rep from * twice more

❀ Fasten off, weave in ends

47 Round Petal Upright Flower

Round 4
Round 3
Round 5

Worked in rounds

❀ MR, ch2, 11tr into ring, join with ss

❀ (ch3, miss 1 st, 1dc in next st) 6 times

❀ (ch3, miss ch3, ss in dc) 6 times

❀ ((ss into next ch3 sp, 5tr, ss) all into ch3 sp) 6 times

❀ ss into ch3 sp of round 2, * 6dtr, ss, all into ch3 sp, ss into next ch3 sp, rep from * 5 times more

❀ Fasten off, weave in ends

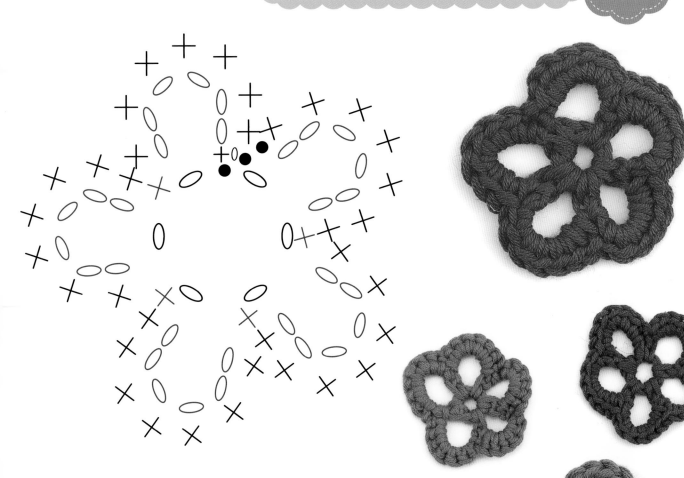

Worked in rounds

❀ ch6, join with ss to make a ring

❀ ch1, (1dc into ring, ch6) 5 times, join with ss in ch1

❀ work 7dc into each ch6 loop of last round, join with ss in first dc

❀ Fasten off, weave in ends

49 Simple Lily

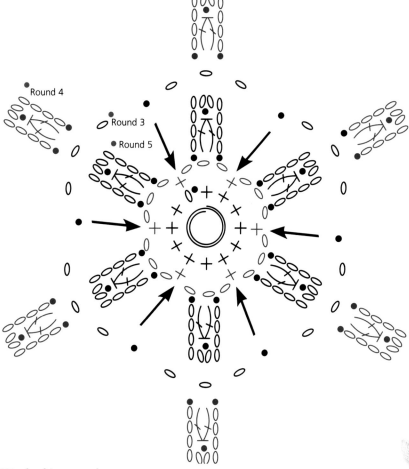

Round 4

Round 3

Round 5

Worked in rounds

❀ MR, ch1, 11dc into ring, join with ss

❀ (ch3, miss 1 st, 1dc in next st) 6 times

❀ (ch3, miss ch3, ss in dc) 6 times

❀ ss into ch3 sp from last round, * (ch4, tr2cl, ch2picot, ch4, ss) all into ch3 sp, ss into next ch3 sp, rep from * 5 times more

❀ ss into ch3 sp from round 2, rep last round working into each ch3 sp

❀ Fasten off, weave in ends

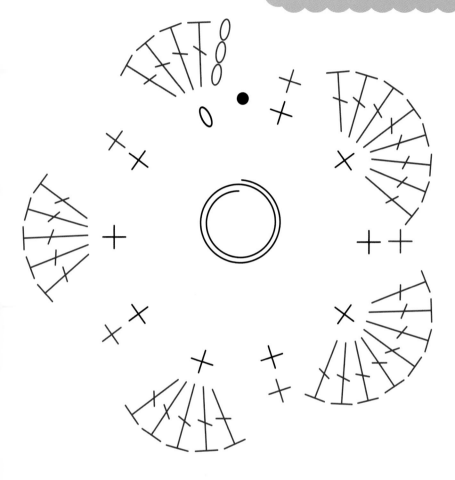

Worked in rounds

❀ in yellow, MR, ch1, 9dc into ring, join with ss, fasten off

❀ join purple, ch3, 4tr in same st, (1dc in next st, 5tr in foll st) twice,
(1dc in next st, 8tr in foll st) twice, 1dc in last st

❀ Fasten off, weave in ends

Small Heart Shaped Leaf

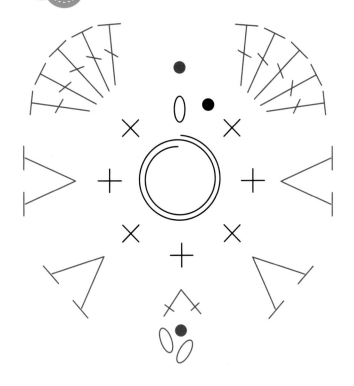

Worked in rounds

❀ MR, ch1, 7dc into ring, join with ss

❀ 5tr in first dc, 2htr in each of next 2 dc, (1dc, ch2picot, 1dc) in next dc, 2htr in each of next 2 dc, 5tr in last dc, join with ss in top of ch1

❀ Fasten off, weave in ends

Square Petal Flower

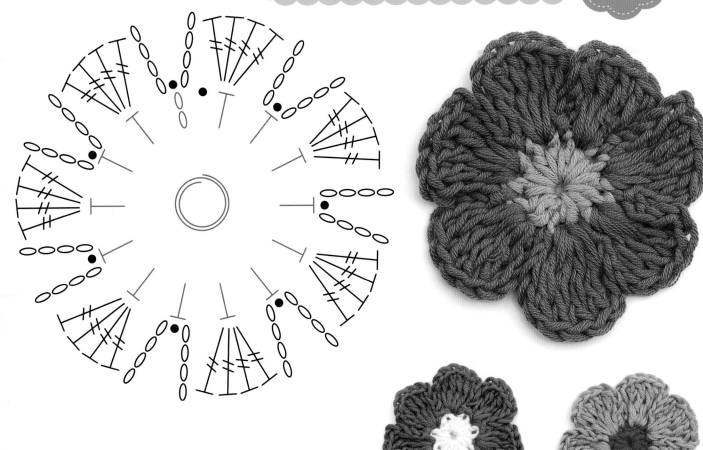

Worked in rounds

❋ in colour A, MR, ch2, 13htr into ring, join with ss, fasten off

❋ join colour B, (ch4, 4dtr in next htr, ch4, ss into next htr) 7 times

❋ Fasten off, weave in ends

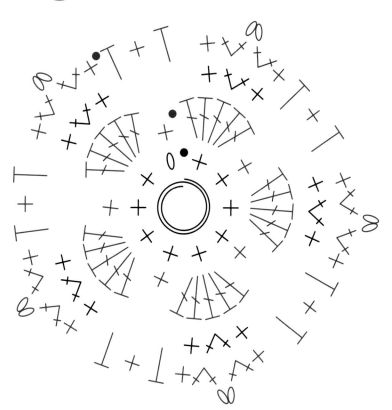

Worked in rounds

❀ holding 1 strand of yellow and 1 strand of pale green together, MR, ch1, 9dc into ring, join with ss, fasten off

❀ join main petal colour, 1dc in same st, 5tr in next st, (1dc in next st, 5tr in foll st) 4 times, join with ss in first dc, fasten off

❀ (join highlight colour in 2nd tr of petal, 1 dc in same st, 2dc in next st, 1dc in foll st, fasten off) 5 times

❀ join the main petal colour to first dc of highlight, (1dc in dc, 2dc in next dc, 2ch, 2dc in next dc, 1dc in next dc, 1htr in tr, 1dc in dc, 1htr in tr) 5 times, join with ss

❀ Fasten off, weave in ends

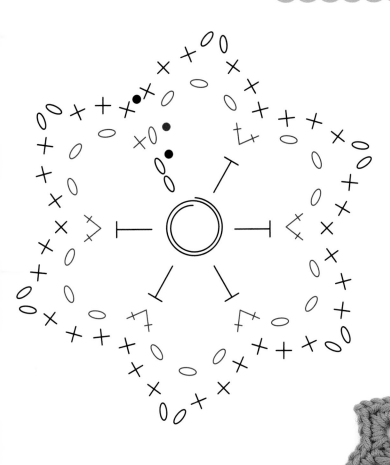

Worked in rounds

❀ MR, ch2, 5htr into ring, join with ss

❀ ch1, 1dc in same st, ch3, (2dc in next htr, ch3) 5 times, join with ss

❀ ((3dc, ch2, 3dc) all into ch3 sp) 6 times, join with ss

❀ Fasten off, weave in ends

Sweet William

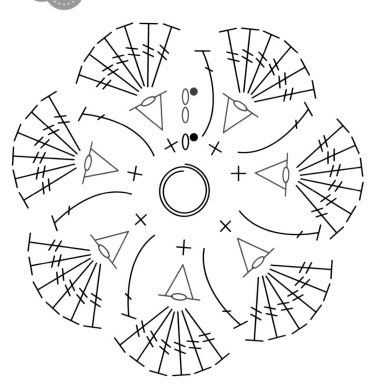

Worked in rounds

❀ in centre colour, MR, ch1, 7dc into ring, join with ss

❀ ch2, (1htr, ch1, 1htr) in each of next 7dc, join with ss in ch2, fasten off

❀ join petal colour in ch1 sp, (6dtr into ch1 sp, tr spike bewteen dcs of round 1) 7 times

❀ Fasten off, weave in ends

Daffodil Small

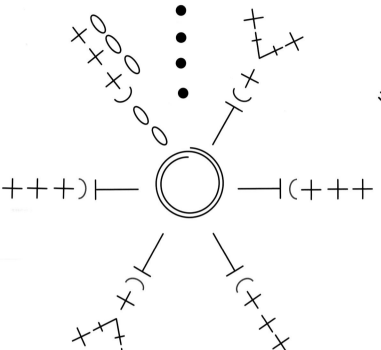

● Petal, work into BLO of htr round 1

Worked in rounds

Trumpet

❈ MR, ch2, 5htr into ring, join with ss

❈ ch1, * 1dc in flo of each htr, rep from * to end, join with ss

❈ ch1, (1dc in each of next 2 sts, 2dc in foll st) twice, join with ss

❈ ch1, 1dc in each dc around, join with ss

❈ Fasten off, weave in ends

Petals

❈ join yellow in any blo of round 1
of trumpet, (ch4, dtr4cl) in blo of htr, fasten off

❈ rep for each petal around trumpet

❈ Weave in ends

Spike Flower Motif

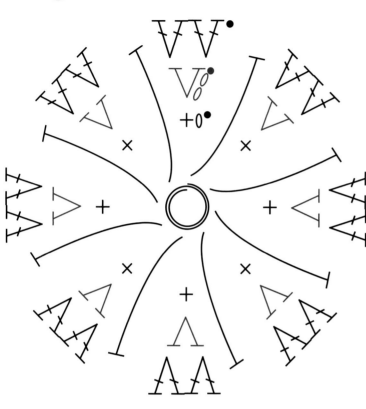

Worked in rounds

❀ in colour A, MR, ch1, 8dc into ring, join with ss, fasten off

❀ join colour B in any dc, ch2, 2htr in same st, (2htr in each dc) 7 times, join with ss in ch2, fasten off

❀ rejoin colour A in any htr, (2tr in each of next 2 htr, htr spike between dcs of round 1) 8 times, join with ss

❀ Fasten off, weave in ends

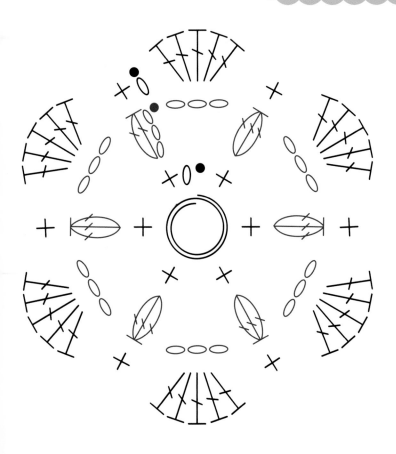

Worked in rounds

❀ in colour A, MR, ch1, 6dc into ring, join with ss, fasten off

❀ join colour B, (ch3, tr2cl) in same dc, ch3, (tr3cl, ch3) 5 times, join with ss in top of first ch3, fasten off

❀ rejoin colour A in top of any tr3cl, ch1, 1dc in same st, 5tr into ch3 sp, (1dc in top of next tr3cl, 5tr into ch3 sp) 5 times, join with ss in first dc

❀ Fasten off, weave in ends

Star Flower Motif

Worked in rounds

❀ MR, ch2, 5htr into ring, join with ss

❀ (ch1, 1dc, ch3, 2dc) all in same st, * ch2, (2dc, ch3, 2dc) all in next htr, rep from * 4 times more, ch2, join with ss in ch1

❀ * (3dc, ch2, 3dc) all into ch3 sp, 1dc into ch2 sp, rep from * 5 times more

❀ Fasten off, weave in ends

Sunflower

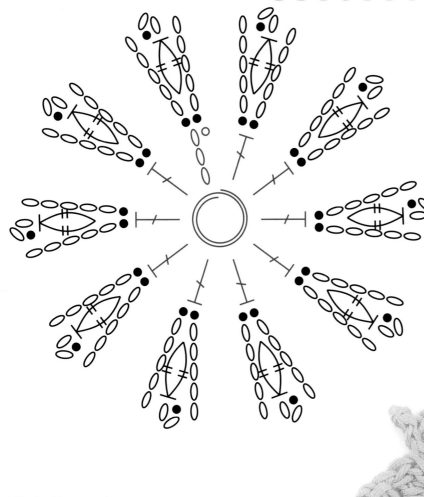

Worked in rounds

❉ in brown, MR, ch3, 9tr into ring, join with ss, fasten off

❉ join yellow with ss in any st, * (ch5, dtr2cl, ch2picot, ch5, ss) all in same st, ss in next tr, rep from * 9 times more

❉ Fasten off, weave in ends

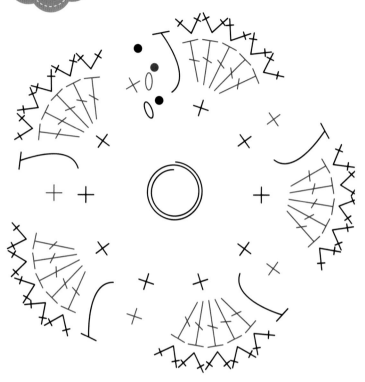

Worked in rounds

❀ in colour A, MR, ch1, 9dc into ring, join with ss, fasten off

❀ join colour B in any st, ch1, 1dc in same st, 5tr in next dc, (1dc in next dc, 5tr in foll dc) 4 times, join with ss in first dc, fasten off

❀ rejoin colour A in first tr of 5tr petal, (2dc in each of next 5 tr, htr spike between dcs of round 1) 5 times, join with ss

❀Fasten off, weave in ends

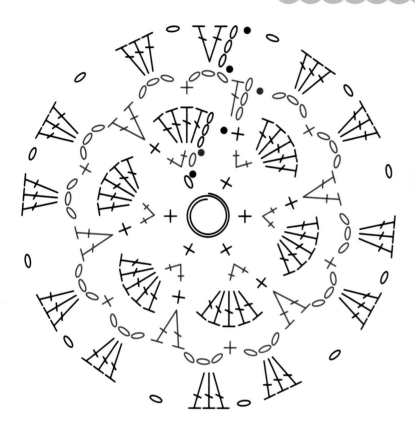

Worked in rounds

❀ in colour A, MR, ch1, 5dc into ring, join with ss

❀ ch1, 2dc in same st, 2dc in each dc around, join with ss, fasten off

❀ join colour B in any dc, ch3, 4tr in same st, 1dc in next dc, (5tr in next dc, 1dc in foll dc) 5 times, join with ss, fasten off

❀ join colour C to any dc, ch3, 1tr in same st, ch3, miss 2 sts, 1dc in 3rd tr or 5tr petal, ch3, miss 2 sts, (2tr in dc, ch3, miss 2 sts, 1dc in 3rd tr of 5tr petal, ch3) 5 times, join with ss in top of ch3

❀ ss into next ch3 sp, (ch3, 2tr) into ch3 sp, ch1, (3tr in ch3 sp, ch1) 11 times, join with ss in top of ch3

❀ Fasten off, weave in ends

Start

Worked in rounds

Rounds 3-5 are worked in BLO.

❀ ch7, make first dc in 2nd ch from hook, 1dc in each of next 4 ch, 4dc in last ch around end, working up opposite side of ch; 1dc in each of next 5ch

❀ ch3, turn, 1dc in blo of same st, 1dc in each blo of next 5 dc, (2dc in blo of next dc, 1dc in blo of foll dc) twice, 1dc in each blo of next 5dc up other side

❀ ch3, turn, 1dc in same st, 1dc in each blo of next 5 dc, 2dc in blo of next dc, 1dc in each blo of next 2 dc, 2dc only in blo of foll dc, 1dc in each blo of next 6 dc

❀ ch3, turn, 1dc in blo of same st, 1dc in each blo of next 6 dc, 2dc in blo of next dc, 1dc in each blo of next 4 dc, 2dc in blo of next dc, 1dc in each blo of next 6 dc, ch3, ss in same st

❀ Fasten off, weave in ends

This simple tulip motif would look striking decorating a bag or even a skirt.
Add some leaves and chain for the stems and make a brightly coloured tulip scene.

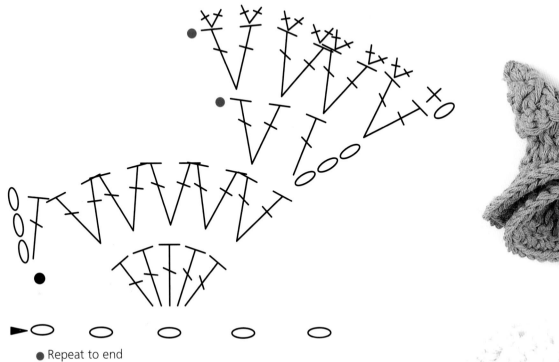

● Repeat to end

Worked in rows

❀ ch5, work 5tr in 3rd ch from hook, ss in last ch, ch3, turn

❀ work 1tr in same st, 2tr in each tr to end, ch3, turn

❀ rep the last row

❀ work 1tr in same st, 2tr in each tr to end, ch1, turn

❀ work 1dc in same st, 2dc in each tr to end

❀ Fasten off, weave in ends

V Shaped Leaf

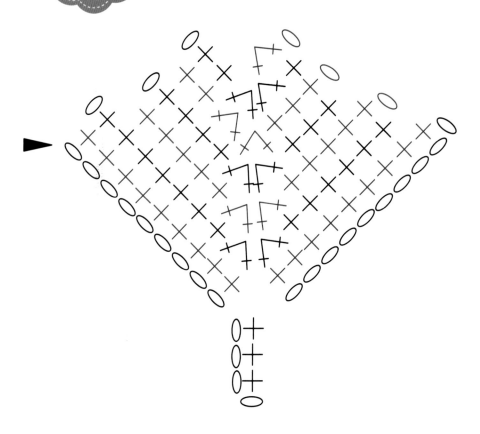

Worked in rounds

❋ ch13, make first dc in 2nd ch from hook, 1dc in each of next 2ch (stem made), ch10

❋ make 1dc in 2nd ch from hook, 1dc in each of next 8 ch, miss stem, 1dc in each of next 9 ch, ch1, turn

❋ 1dc in each of next 7 dc, (dc2tog) twice, 1dc in each of next 6 dc, ch1, turn

❋ 1dc in each of next 5 dc, (dc2tog) twice, 1dc in each of next 5 dc, ch1, turn

❋ 1dc in each of next 4 dc, (dc2tog) twice, 1dc in each of next 3 dc, ch1, turn

❋ 1dc in each of next 3 dc, (dc2tog) twice, 1dc in each of next 2 dc, ch1, turn

❋ 1dc in each of next 2 dc, (dc2tog) twice, 1dc in next dc, ch1, turn

❋ dc2tog

❋ Fasten off, weave in ends

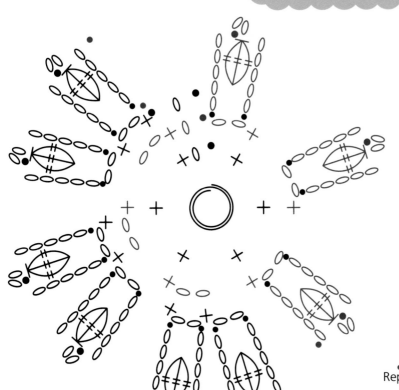

Repeat to end

Worked in rounds

❀ MR, ch1, 6dc into ring, join with ss

❀ ch1, 1dc in same st, ch2, (1dc in dc, ch2) 5 times, join with ss

❀ ch1, 1dc in same st, (ch2, 1dc, ch2) all into ch2 sp, * 1dc in dc, (ch2, 1dc, ch2) all into ch2 sp, rep from * 5 times more, ss into ch2 sp of round 2

❀ * (ch5, dtr3cl, ch2picot, ch5, ss) all into ch2 sp of round 2, ss in next ch2 sp of round 2, rep from * 5 times more, ss into ch2 sp of round 3

❀ * (ch5, dtr3cl, ch2picot, ch5, ss) all into ch2 sp of round 3, ss in next ch2 sp, rep from * 11 times more

❀ Fasten off, weave in ends

STEP BY STEP
TECHNIQUES

Chain (ch)

Chains are used as a starting base for your work and, in this book, to work stitches into and around. You will be directed to crochet along the edge of the chain, crocheting through the top loop of each chain stitch, and down the opposite side of the chain in the loop on the other side of each chain stitch. I have used this technique for leaves and some petals. Another way of working with a chain is to crochet into a chain space, chain loop or chain ring. In this case you will work around the chain and not into individual chain stitches. This technique has been used for petals and as an alternative to a magic ring at the start of a flower.

When crocheting into a chain you will be directed to insert your hook into the 2nd, 3rd or 4th chain from hook depending on whether you are working double crochet, half treble or treble stitches as this is to give enough height for the subsequent stitches.

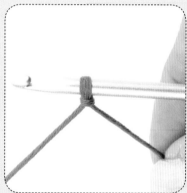  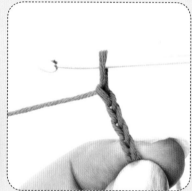

1. Make a slip knot in the yarn, leaving a long enough tail to sew in later. Put slip knot on hook and tighten it to fit hook.

2. Yarn round hook, pull the yarn through the loop on the hook to form one chain.

3. Repeat step 2 until the correct number of chain stitches have been made.

Double Crochet (along a chain)

1. Insert hook into directed stitch and wrap yarn round hook.

2. Pull yarn through stitch to front of crochet. 2 loops on hook.

3. Yarn round hook again.

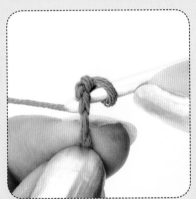

4. Pull yarn through both loops on hook.

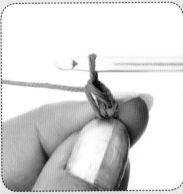

5. Double crochet made. You will always start and finish a double crochet with 1 loop on your hook.

6. Finished row of double crochet worked into a chain.

Working DC Along the Opposite Side of the Chain

1. To 'turn the corner' I have worked 3 double crochet in the last chain and turned the work so I am ready to work from right to left along the opposite side loops of the chain.

2. Insert hook in the loop on the other side of the chain. Once you have turned the work, these loops will be along the top of the chain.

3. Double crochet worked along the top of the chain, the corner turned and double crochet worked along the opposite side of the chain.

Alternative to a Magic Ring – chain ring

1. Work chain in normal way then insert hook into the first chain made (furthest from hook).

2. Yarn round hook and pull through 2 loops on hook.

3. Slip stitch made joining the two ends of the chain together to form a ring.

4. Work into the ring as follows: insert the hook through the ring from front to back. Yarn round hook and pull through to front of ring. Complete the stitch as instructed.

Magic Ring (MR)

I use the magic ring technique frequently in the book as it gives you a starting ring for a flower that you are in control of. If the centre is too tight for the stitches, ease the ring out a little. If the circle is too loose, pull on the free yarn end to close the ring.

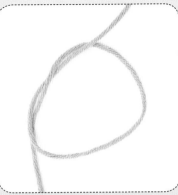

1. Make a loop in the yarn as if you were going to tie a knot but without pulling it tight.

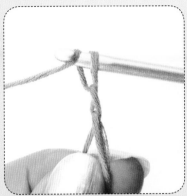

2. Gripping the join in the loop with your left hand, insert hook through loop from front to back. Wrap yarn round hook and pull through loop. Yarn round hook again.

3. Pull yarn through loop on hook to form first stitch.

4. Continue to work stitches into ring as instructed.

Double Crochet (dc) +

Working dc into magic ring

1. Make a magic ring as instructed.

2. Insert hook in ring from front to back. Wrap yarn round hook.

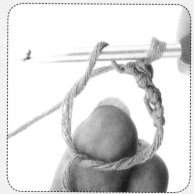

3. Pull the yarn through the ring to the front. 2 loops on hook.

4. Yarn round hook again.

5. Pull the yarn through both loops on hook. Double crochet made.

6. Work the instructed number of stitches in the same way then gently pull the tail end of yarn to close the ring a little.

The number of chain needed at the beginning of working in a magic ring depends on the stitch used. For double crochet; chain 1, for half treble; chain 2, for treble; chain 3 and so on.

7. Magic ring closed a little.

8. Magic ring closed fully.

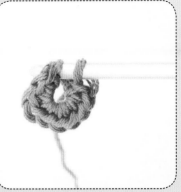

9. Insert the hook in the top of the first double crochet you made.

10. Yarn round hook and pull through the top of the double crochet and the loop on the hook. Slip stitch made.

11. This closes the circle of stitches worked into the magic ring. Pull on the tail end of yarn again to tighten the ring further if needed.

Double Crochet Two Together (dc2tog) ⟋⟍⤬

This is a method of decreasing or shaping by working two double crochet stitches together to form one stitch.

1. Insert hook into stitch, yarn round hook and pull through to front of work. 2 loops on hook. Do not complete the double crochet in the same way.

2. Instead, insert the hook into the next stitch, yarn round hook and pull through to front of work. 3 loops now on hook.

3. Yarn round hook.

4. Pull yarn through all 3 loops on hook. 1 loop remains on hook and dc2tog has been made.

Chain 3 Picot (ch3picot)

1. Chain 3.

2. Insert hook into the 3rd chain from hook.

3. Yarn round hook.

4. Pull through both loops on hook. Picot made.

5. Picots are used to give a pointed tip to the motif.

Chain 2 Picot (ch2picot)

1. Chain 2
2. Insert hook into the 2nd chain from hook
3. Yarn round hook
4. Pull through both loops on hook. Picot made

Back Loop Only (blo) ⌢

1. The stitches are worked in the usual way, but only through the back loop of the stitch rather than both loops as is usual.

Front Loop Only (flo) ⌣

1. The stitches are worked in the usual way, but only through the front loop of the stitch rather than both loops as is usual.

Half Treble Crochet (htr) T

1. Yarn round hook.

2. Insert hook in stitch, yarn round hook again.

3. Pull yarn through to front of work. 3 loops on hook.

4. Yarn round hook once more.

5. Pull yarn through all 3 loops on hook. Half treble made.

Half Treble Spike (htrsp) $\rfloor$

1. Yarn round hook.

2. Insert hook into the directed stitch and row.

3. Yarn round hook and pull through to front of work.

4. 3 loops on hook.

5. Yarn round hook.

6. Pull yarn through all 3 loops.

7. Half treble spike made.

Treble Crochet (tr)

1. Yarn round hook.

2. Insert hook in stitch.

3. Yarn round hook.

4. Pull yarn through to front of work. 3 loops on hook.

5. Yarn round hook.

6. Pull through first 2 loops, leaving 2 loops on hook.

7. Yarn round hook once more.

8. Pull through remaining 2 loops leaving 1 loop on hook. Treble crochet made.

Treble Spike (trsp)

1. Yarn round hook.

2. Insert hook in stitch and row from front to back and push hook throg to back.

3. Yarn round hook.

4. Pull yarn through to front. 3 loops on hook.

5. Yarn round hook.

6. Pull through first 2 loops leaving 2 loops on hook.

7. Yarn round hook.

8. Pull through both loops on hook. Treble spike made.

Treble 2 Cluster (tr3cl)

1. Yarn round hook.

2. Insert hook into stitch.

3. Yarn round hook and pull through to front of work. 3 loops on hook.

4. Yarn round hook and pull through first 2 loops on hook.

5. Leaving 2 loops on hook.

6. Yarn round hook.

7. Insert hook into same stitch as before.

8. Yarn round hook and pull through to front of work. 4 loops now on hook.

9. Yarn round hook and pull through first 2 loops on hook.

10. Leaving 3 loops on hook.

11. Yarn round hook.

12. Pull yarn through all 3 loops on hook.

13. Leaving 1 loop on hook.

14. Yarn round hook once more.

15. Pull through to secure stitch. Treble 2 cluster made.

Treble 3 Cluster and Treble 5 Cluster

To work a Treble 3 Cluster (tr3cluster) and Treble 5 Cluster (tr5cluster), repeat steps 6, 7, 8 and 9 until the correct number of trebles have been made and the last loop of each one (plus the starting loop from the previous stitch) are all on the hook (4 loops for tr3cluster, 6 loops for tr5cluster) then work steps 11, 12, 13, 14 and 15 to complete the cluster.

Popcorn (pc)

1. Popcorn is worked in 1 stitch.

2. Work 5 treble crochet in 1 stitch.

3. Remove the hook from the final stitch leaving a big loop.

4. Insert the hook into the top of the first of the 5 treble crochet you worked.

5. Put the loop from the last stitch back on the hook.

6. Pull the last stitch through the top of the first teble to front of work.

7. 1 loop on hook.

8. Yarn round hook once more.

9. Pull yarn through to secure the stitch.

10. Popcorn made.

Double Treble Crochet (dtr)

1. Wrap yarn round hook twice.

2. Insert hook in stitch, wrap yarn round hook again.

3. Pull yarn through stitch to front of work. 4 loops on hook.

4. Yarn round hook.

5. Pull yarn through first 2 loops on hook. 3 loops now on hook.

6. Wrap yarn round hook again and pull through first 2 loops on hook. 2 loops now on hook.

7. Wrap yarn round hook once more and pull through both loops on hook. Double treble crochet made.

Double Treble 2 Cluster (dtr2cl)

Work the required number of double treble stitches all in the same instructed stitch (2 here), leaving the last loop of each one on the hook. Then wrap yarn round hook and pull through all loops on hook (3 here). Wrap yarn round hook once more and pull through to secure the cluster.

Double Treble 3 Cluster (dtr3cl)

Work the required number of double treble stitches all in the same instructed stitch (3 here), leaving the last loop of each one on the hook. Then wrap yarn round hook and pull through all loops on hook (4 here). Wrap yarn round hook once more and pull through to secure the cluster.

Double Treble 4 Cluster (dtr4cl)

Work the required number of double treble stitches all in the same instructed stitch (4 here), leaving the last loop of each one on the hook. Then wrap yarn round hook and pull through all loops on hook (5 here). Wrap yarn round hook once more and pull through to secure the cluster.

Double Treble 5 Cluster (dtr5cl)

Work the required number of double treble stitches all in the same instructed stitch (5 here), leaving the last loop of each one on the hook. Then wrap yarn round hook and pull through all loops on hook (6 here). Wrap yarn round hook once more and pull through to secure the cluster.

Triple Treble Crochet (trtr)

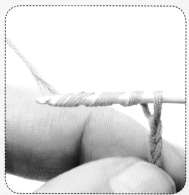

1. Wrap yarn round hook three times and insert hook in instructed stitch.

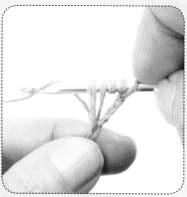

2. Wrap yarn round hook and pull through to front. 5 loops on hook. Yarn round hook and pull through first 2 loops. 4 loops now on hook.

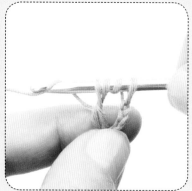

3. Wrap yarn round hook and pull through first 2 loops. 3 loops now on hook. Yarn round hook and pull through first 2 loops. 2 loops on hook.

4. Wrap yarn round hook and pull through final 2 loops. Triple treble complete.

Crocheting Around a Wire Stem

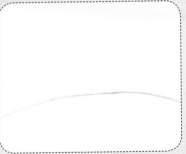

1. Fold the ends of the wire to make a place to attach the yarn and so any sharp cut ends are hidden.

2. Attach the yarn and work double crochet around the stem in the same way you would work into a magic ring or chain space. You can bend the wire to make it easier to work around.

3. Continue working dc along the stem, making sure the stem is covered.

4. Attach the flowers, by tying or stitching them into place, any knots will be covered by the crochet on the stem.

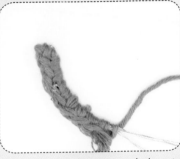

5. You can use the same technique to quickly create leaves.

6. Crochet around the leaf shaped wire in the same way, joining with a ss at the end.

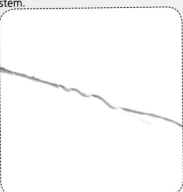

7. Another easy method is to attach the yarn in the same way and then wrap the yarn around the wire stem until it is covered.

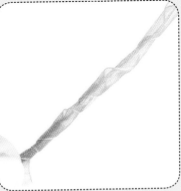

8. If you are creating a large bouquet of crochet flowers for display in a vase where the stems will be mainly hidden, you can use stretchy florists tape to cover the wire. Simply attach and wrap the tape in the same way.

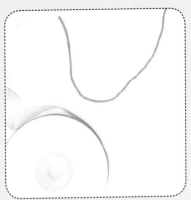

9. You could also use green florists wire or pipe cleaners for the stems.

IDEAS

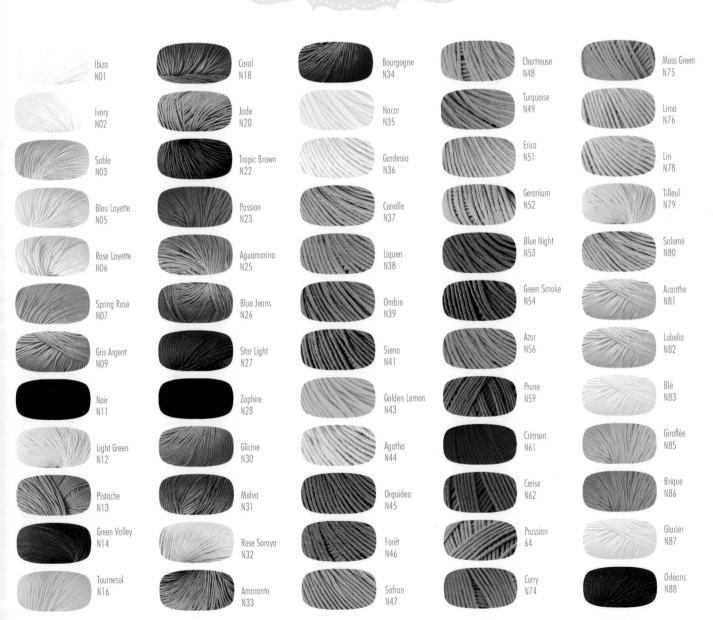

Natura
Colour Card

Ibiza N01	Coral N18	Bourgogne N34
Ivory N02	Jade N20	Nacar N35
Sable N03	Tropic Brown N22	Gardenia N36
Bleu Layette N05	Passion N23	Canelle N37
Rose Layette N06	Aguamarina N25	Liquen N38
Spring Rose N07	Blue Jeans N26	Ombre N39
Gris Argent N09	Star Light N27	Siena N41
Noir N11	Zaphire N28	Golden Lemon N43
Light Green N12	Glicine N30	Agatha N44
Pistache N13	Malva N31	Orquidea N45
Green Valley N14	Rose Soraya N32	Forêt N46
Tournesol N16	Amaranto N33	Safran N47

Chartreuse N48	Moss Green N75
Turquoise N49	Lima N76
Erica N51	Lin N78
Geranium N52	Tilleul N79
Blue Night N53	Salomé N80
Green Smoke N54	Acanthe N81
Azur N56	Lobelia N82
Prune N59	Blé N83
Crimson N61	Giroflée N85
Cerise N62	Brique N86
Prussian 64	Glacier N87
Curry N74	Orléans N88